Education Matters

Jenna Dellaccio

PowerKiDS press

Published in 2025 by The Rosen Publishing Group, Inc.
2544 Clinton Street, Buffalo, NY 14224

Copyright © 2025 by The Rosen Publishing Group, Inc.

All rights reserved. No part of this book may be reproduced in any form without permission in writing from the publisher, except by a reviewer.

Editor: Michele Suchomel-Casey
Book Design: Leslie Taylor

Photo Credits: Cover, pp. 19, 21 wavebreakmedia/Shutterstock.com; (series background) P.siripak/Shutterstock.com; (series disability pride colors) rudall30/Shutterstock.com; p. 5 wee dezign/Shutterstock.com, (flag sidebar) Maxim Studio/Shutterstock.com; p. 7 Tada Images/Shutterstock.com; pp. 9, 17 Pressmaster/Shutterstock.com; p. 11 Reshetnikov_art/Shutterstock.com; p. 13 Media_Photos/Shutterstock.com; p. 14 wavebreakmedia/Shutterstock.com; p. 15 Taylordw/WikiCommons: File:2019-Jul-25-TASH-OLDL-Judy-Heumann.jpg.

Cataloging-in-Publication Data

Names: Tolli, Jenna.
Title: Education matters / Jenna Dellaccio.
Description: Buffalo, NY : PowerKids Press, 2025. | Series: Disability pride | Includes glossary and index.
Identifiers: ISBN 9781499446746 (pbk.) | ISBN 9781499446753 (library bound) | ISBN 9781499446760 (ebook)
Subjects: LCSH: Children with disabilities–Education–Law and legislation–United States–Juvenile literature. | Children with disabilities–Education–Juvenile literature. | People with disabilities–Civil rights–Juvenile literature.
Classification: LCC KF4210.T65 2025 | DDC 344.73'07911–dc23

Manufactured in the United States of America

Some of the images in this book illustrate individuals who are models. The depictions do not imply actual situations or events.

CPSIA Compliance Information: Batch #CSPK25. For Further Information contact Rosen Publishing at 1-800-237-9932.

Contents

Education for Everyone 4
Disability Rights Laws 6
Specific Learning Disabilities 8
Accessibility in Schools 10
Individualized Education Program 12
Integrated Classrooms 14
Facing Challenges 16
Be an Ally 18
Disability Rights in Education 20
Glossary 22
For More Information 23
Index 24

Education for Everyone

Did you know that over 7 million students in U.S. public schools have a disability? A disability is a physical or mental **impairment** that can make it harder to do certain activities. There are lots of ways that teachers and parents have made learning with disabilities easier for students.

It's important for everyone to receive an education. A disability can affect how someone attends school and interacts in the classroom. Sometimes disabilities affect the way someone learns or the way they **process** information. They might have trouble with listening, speaking, reading, writing, **reasoning**, or doing math.

The disability pride flag was created to show acceptance and respect for people who have disabilities. Each color is for a different type of disability.

- The gray background is in honor of those who've died.
- Green is for disabilities that have to do with the senses.
- Blue is for those that have to with the mind and emotions.
- White stands for unseen disabilities, as well as those that haven't been diagnosed, or found out.
- Gold is for neurodiversity.
- Red is for other disabilities of the body.

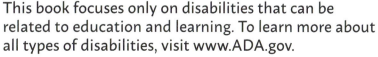

This book focuses only on disabilities that can be related to education and learning. To learn more about all types of disabilities, visit www.ADA.gov.

Disability Rights Laws

In 1975, a law was passed to give all children with disabilities the right to a free public education. This law is now known as the Individuals with Disabilities Education Act, or the IDEA. It protects students' rights in school, no matter what disability or need they may have.

The IDEA says that education should be provided in the "least **restrictive environment**" for students. This means classrooms should be **inclusive** as much as possible.

The Americans with Disabilities Act (ADA) was passed in 1990. It protects individuals with disabilities from being treated unfairly throughout their lives, including at school and at their jobs.

Children Helped by IDEA

Academic Year	Number of Students Served
1990-1991	4.7 million
2000-2001	6.3 million
2010-2011	6.4 million
2020-2021	7.2 million

The number of children in the United States who receive services under the IDEA has gone up over the years.

The U.S. Department of Education is in charge of federal **policies**, research, financial aid, equal access for students, and other education issues.

Specific Learning Disabilities

There are certain challenges people may have that affect how they learn and understand information. Here are a few examples of learning disorders:

Dyslexia is when someone has trouble reading and processing language. People with dyslexia can find it hard to remember details of things that they read, or they might struggle when they sound out words. It's the most common learning disability.

Dyscalculia is when someone has a hard time understanding math. People with dyscalculia might have trouble learning to count or remembering numbers.

Dysgraphia is when someone has trouble with writing. They might also struggle with grammar and spelling.

Not everyone who has trouble learning has a disability. Lots of students need extra help at different times or in certain academic subjects.

Learn More

Other conditions, such as attention deficit hyperactivity disorder (ADHD), can also affect learning. ADHD isn't a learning disability, but it can make focusing in school harder. Visit ADD.org or CHADD.org to learn more.

Accessibility in Schools

Some people have disabilities related to their ability to hear, see, or get around. They may use certain tools to help them with **accessibility**. These tools could include hearing aids, wheelchairs, crutches, or other kinds of equipment.

Sometimes there are physical **barriers** that limit accessibility to a place or to **resources**. Schools have to make sure they're accessible to everyone. This can mean having a ramp that is not too steep outside and elevators to move around in a building. Having accessible restrooms and doors that can be easily opened without twisting a knob or handle are other examples.

Assistive devices in classrooms can make education more accessible. This is a photo of a braille keyboard, which can be used by people who have a visual impairment.

Learn More

A recent survey found that more than half of U.S. public schools have accessibility barriers. This makes it challenging or even impossible for people with disabilities to access those schools safely.

Individualized Education Program

Everyone should be able to learn in the way that works best for them. An Individualized Education Program, or IEP, is a documented plan that parents and teachers create for students who have disabilities. Each plan is designed for a specific student's needs.

Creating an IEP can help to outline what someone's strengths are and what they might have a harder time learning in school. It includes the student's current level of education, goals for their education, and services they will receive to help them learn. For example, depending on the student's disability, they may be given additional time to take tests.

An IEP team includes the student, a parent or guardian, a special education teacher, a regular education teacher, and someone from the school district.

Integrated Classrooms

Before the IDEA became law, students with disabilities would often be separated from classmates without disabilities.

Integrated classrooms are places where all students, those who have disabilities and those who do not, learn together in one classroom. This learning environment is much more common today. It has been found to have better outcomes, or results, for students.

The IDEA was a big reason for this change. It required schools to make the best possible **accommodations** for all of their students to help their education. Today, many students with disabilities spend the majority of their time in general classes.

Judith Heumann was a disability rights leader and **activist** known throughout the world. She fought for students with disabilities to have equal rights.

Facing Challenges

Students who have disabilities are more likely to drop out of school compared to their peers who do not have disabilities. This can be related to barriers in the school system, which may treat students with disabilities in an unequal way compared to their peers.

Schools might have limited funding that can affect the resources students need. A lack of training for teachers on disability education can also be a challenge.

School discipline is another barrier. Overall, the number of students being suspended and expelled (kicked out) from school has gone up. It has been found that students with disabilities are suspended more often than their peers.

If you or a friend is having trouble in school or is being treated unfairly, talk with a trusted parent or teacher. They will find resources to help and will work with you.

Learn More

Challenges in school can lead to challenges in adult life. Students from different backgrounds and of different abilities can be treated unfairly and face more legal problems.

Be an Ally

We should all feel included, accepted, and valued. Students can also learn better when they are supported and feel safe in school. Understanding that we all have different needs is one way you can support your peers who have disabilities. You can be an **ally** by learning about disabilities and respecting everyone.

The words you use to talk to your peers about disabilities are very important. Person-first language is one way to be inclusive and respectful. This means referring to a person themself before the disability they may have. It includes using terms like "people with disabilities" instead of "disabled people."

Sometimes it's hard to know the right words to say. It's OK to ask questions when you are confused, but always make sure to respect others' feelings.

If you hear someone in your class being disrespectful, be sure to tell a teacher. One of the best ways to be an ally is by sticking up for others.

Disability Rights in Education

About one in every four people in the United States has a disability. This may be a learning disability, a physical or mental disability, or another challenge that can affect someone's life and education.

Making sure everyone has the resources they need to succeed in school is not only the goal for teachers and parents, it's part of the law in our country. There have been many advances in disability rights, but there's always more work to do.

Learn More

Always remember that every person experiences the world in their own way. Disabilities can affect everyone differently.

By being respectful of our peers and understanding disabilities in education, we can all work together to make schools more inclusive.

You can learn how to support disability rights by visiting the National Center for Learning Disabilities website at NCLD.org, or the American Civil Liberties Union website at ACLU.org.

Glossary

accessibility: The quality of being easy to use or understand.

accommodation: Something that is supplied to meet someone's needs.

activist: Someone who acts strongly in support of or against an issue.

ally: A person who stands up for fairness and wants to learn about what they can do to help make sure everyone is treated equally.

barrier: Something that blocks something from passing.

environment: The things and conditions that are all around a person.

impairment: Loss of function or ability.

inclusive: Including everyone or covering everything.

integrate: To help a person or group to become part of a larger group.

policy: A law that people use to help them make decisions.

process: To think about and understand the meaning of something.

reasoning: Process of forming conclusions or judgments.

resource: Something that helps or supports.

restrictive: Limiting or controlling.

For More Information

BOOKS

Cocca-Leffler, Maryann. *Fighting for Yes! The Story of Disability Rights Activist Judith Heumann.* New York, NY: Abrams Books for Young Readers, 2022.

Cocca-Leffler, Maryann, and Janine Leffler. *We Want to Go to School!* Chicago, IL: Albert Whitman & Company, 2021.

Wong, Alice. *Disability Visibility: 17 First-Person Stories for Today: Adapted for Young Adults.* New York, NY: Ember, Random House Children's Books, 2021.

WEBSITES

The American Civil Liberties Union (ACLU)
www.aclu.org
The ACLU is a human rights organization that focuses on protecting rights and liberties for everyone in the United States.

National Center for Learning Disabilities
www.ncld.org
This website provides news, resources, data, and activities to take action on learning disabilities.

U.S. Department of Justice Civil Rights Division, Americans with Disabilities Act (ADA)
www.ada.gov
Check out this site to find information and resources related to the ADA for those with disabilities, along with guidance on how to file an ADA complaint.

Publisher's note to educators and parents: Our editors have carefully reviewed these websites to ensure that they are suitable for students. Many websites change frequently, however, and we cannot guarantee that a site's future contents will continue to meet our high standards of quality and educational value. Be advised that students should be closely supervised whenever they access the internet.

Index

A
Americans with Disabilities Act (ADA), 6
attention deficit hyperactivity disorder (ADHD), 9

B
braille, 11

D
devices, 10, 11
disability pride flag, 5
discipline, 16, 17
dyscalculia, 8
dysgraphia, 8
dyslexia, 8

H
Heumann, Judith, 15

I
Individualized Education Plan (IEP), 12, 13
Individuals with Disabilities Education Act (IDEA), 6, 7, 14, 15

M
math, 4, 8

P
parents, 4, 12, 13, 17, 20

person-first language, 18

R
reading, 4, 8
respect, 5, 18, 19, 21
rights, 6, 15, 20, 21

T
teachers, 4, 12, 13, 16, 17, 19, 20

U
U.S. Department of Education, 7

W
wheelchairs, 10
writing, 4, 8